Budget Management

Easy Techniques to Keep Your Finances and Budget Under Control

I0483954

Financial Learning Series

Dueep J. Singh

Mendon Cottage Books

JD-Biz Publishing

Disclaimer

The information is this book is provided for informational purposes only. It is not intended to be used and medical advice or a substitute for proper medical treatment by a qualified health care provider. The information is believed to be accurate as presented based on research by the author.

The contents have not been evaluated by the U.S. Food and Drug Administration or any other Government or Health Organization and the contents in this book are not to be used to treat cure or prevent disease.

The author or publisher is not responsible for the use or safety of any diet, procedure or treatment mentioned in this book. The author or publisher is not responsible for errors or omissions that may exist.

Warning

The Book is for informational purposes only and before taking on any diet, treatment or medical procedure, it is recommended to consult with your primary health care provider.

Our books are available at

1. Amazon.com
2. Barnes and Noble
3. Itunes
4. Kobo
5. Smashwords
6. Google Play Books

Table of Contents

Introduction

There was a time when managing finances for the family was considered to be a part of every future homemakers' training. A girl had to learn to become up proper and capable household manager and utilize all the finances available to her in a sensible and adept manner. The world economy in itself means the careful use of available materials, including money.

A large majority of women have charge of the spending of most of the money gained by the wage earners of the family. So if the woman is extravagant and has no economic sense, the family is soon going to find itself facing a number of bills on the 1st of every month, adding to the stack of unpaid bills from the previous month.

Let us take an example – what is going to benefit the family more, an increase of hundred dollars in your annual income, or the saving of the same amount by wise management? You may think a penny saved is a penny earned as one of the old-time clichés, but our ancestors went through hard economic and financial times. They knew how to stretch a dollar so far that it squeaked.

The Great Depression of the 1930s is now the Great Depression of the 2020s, and the financial and economic problems, which took place then are still very much around. So a little bit of sensible management, proper judgment and some self-discipline is going to help you in managing expenditure properly so that you never have spent nights wondering where you are going to get enough of money to pay pending and long-overdue bills.

Budget management is not a modern concept. It started in the 1880s under the label of home economics in the USA when it was taught to girls at school who were the future homemakers. Cornell University is the only universe to the USA, which had a full-fledged curriculum based on home economics.

In the 1880s, the topics taught were limited to the purchase of food, nutrition, go query, clothing, suing, choice of textiles, and household equipment. Along with that, housecleaning, housing, hygiene and household economics was taught as a domestic science.

Home economics at that time and later, soon began to include the maniac acts of any relations, parental education, consumer education and institutional management to home economy until now in the 21st century, the application of scientific techniques when applied to home economy is being studied and developed.

This is focusing mainly on the economic, social and aesthetic aspects of building a home, and managing it properly.

In many countries, this subject is known as Home Science Domestic Science, domestic economy or household arts – whatever the label, the information is going to the same, because all these topics are universal and they need to be dealt with through scientific and common sense methods.

Prof. Joan Brumberg who is a professor in human development and A Stephen H. Weiss Presidential Fellow describes home economics as being one of the major pathways for women into public education in the late 19 and early 20th Centuries, providing entry to a wide variety of careers for women in business, Academia, public education, healthcare and government up to the 1960s.

Naturally feminists in the 1960s and 70s did not support this information and knowledge pertaining to domesticity, because according to them, anything that smacked of domesticity was considered to be a shackle on women's opportunities! However, in the 1990s, feminist scholars in the West,-including the USA – decided that yes, home economics was something with meaning, providing opportunities to American women, both inside the home and outside it.

So as financial management and budgeting is a part of home economics, you are now going to get to know how is it is to make a budget, keep within it, and find your financial burdens easing off.

Thinking up a Budget

Wow! So what do I buy right away?

There are some important parts which you need to understand when making up a budget. How much of money do you have right at hand. The first question is to make up a list of your top priorities. How many portions are you going to divide that particular amount into? The 2nd part is to decide what proportion is going to be spent for each particular portion or division of your budget.

There are some expenses which are static. These are going to occur every month regardless of whether you have money enough to pay for them or not. These include the bills for food, shelter, and services related bills like electricity and water.

The rest of the expenditures can be called floating expenditures. These are not the bare necessities and statics, but the incidentals for which you have to spend money as and when necessary and when required.

These extra expenditures are going to include travel costs, education, amusement, entertainment, loans, and mortgage repayments and paying of premiums like life insurance. These are fluctuating expenditures which you may or may not have, but they are going to make major inroads into your monthly budget.

Clothing comes next. You do not buy clothes every month, do you, unless you are a neurotic /obsessive compulsive buyer or chronic shopaholic. Under such circumstances, you are not going to stay within a budget because the next time you see a discount sale, you are going to go compulsively right into the shop and forget about the budget.

You can call all of these additional operating expenses. The amount of money which is going to be spent under each head is going to depend on the amount of the income coming in, the members of the family and the style or the standard of living.

This last item is where you need to have a realistic outlook. You do not follow million-dollar lifestyle, if the income that is coming in can be counted in thousands. That is when you have to make sure that you use some sense and do not try keeping up with the Jonases just out of a matter of pride. Most of the discontent felt by people today is because they aspire to so many things without having the means of getting them. But that this is a natural instinct – even King Ahab coveted the vineyard of Naboth.

But you are definitely not a king with all his different flows of income coming over tomorrow directions. You have a limited number of income sources. If your income is small, a very large percentage of it is going to be spent on food. On the other hand, you should know how much proportion of your income should you spend on food, depending on your income.

For example, if you have just 300 – $500 coming in this week/month, a major portion of it is going to be utilized in paying your food bills. But if you have an income, where you just put in one number and forget the zeros coming behind it, you are definitely not going to bother about how much percentage you spend on food.

That is why you need to make up a realistic list of the items which your family needs in the category of food. Now put that some under the head of "food" in your budget.

Money for shelter is also going to vary. If you are renting out your accommodation, you will need to pay a fixed amount in-house rent every month. You may also have to pay a mortgage payment, if applicable. Food and shelter bills take up almost the entire income, leaving just a little for clothing. If you live in your own house estimate the interest on the sum of money invested in your house. Add to it, insurance, taxes, water rates, electricity rates and whatever expenses are made in keeping your property in a good condition.

Consider this amount as the cost of your shelter and enter it under the heading of "Shelter" in your budget.

If you have your own house, the interest on the investment in it is going to be added to your income before you find the percentage of the total income, which goes for the various items of the budget. This interest is miniscule. So looking at your finances, you may want to look at an option of – could you live in a smaller house if you did all your own work? You could put out this house to rent. This unfortunately is not an option for a large percentage of us, because we do not have ready-made houses right at hand to rent out and thus increase our income.

It is also not good economy to try to save some money by living in a smaller house, doing your own work, and saving pennies if it is at the cost of your health. This is penny wise pound foolish because the amount of money that you are going to waste in doctor's bills down the line because you have shifted to an insalubrious neighborhood is going to put paid to a methodically thought of budget.

Now we come to operating expenses. These are the expenses which are going to be incurred for household and personal use. This is the amount which you are going to spend sensibly, and depending on necessity, social requirement, climate, income, and even good taste. Let us put clothing under this heading.

Dressing comfortably in a warm climate is not expensive. However, expenses for clothing increase in cold atmospheres. You may also want to invest in a business attire depending on your profession. A plumber can get away with casual wear, but a doctor has to be formally dressed because he knows how a patient needs the aura of serious professionalism to reassure him.

Good taste in dress is good economy. Much of the money wasted on clothes is spent by those who do not stop to think whether the clothes selected are what you need. You saw it shining, beckoning and enticing in the shop. You saw other people saying ooooh, that is so stylish. So you went and maxed your credit card to buy something you would possibly never wear, but hey, somebody else wanted it so you got in first…

Make a list of how much you spend on clothing. How much does your family spend on necessary/unnecessary clothing? Cut down on those futile spending sprees.

The third point, which we are going to tackle now is Keeping up with the Joneses. Food, clothing and shelter has been taken care of. Now we are going to concentrate on the all too human desire to make a splash in society. These are more than basic comforts. People living on a limited budget can make do with free entertainment, but the wealthy have many entertainment items to enter under this particular head. This includes social entertaining for business reasons. For an average income, the amount which you are going to spend on this particular field is going to largely depend upon your self-control, and the good management shown in your expenditure for food, clothing and shelter.

If anybody remembers Paul Gallico's *Mrs. 'Arris goes to Paris*, it is the story of a London charwoman who decides to buy a Dior dress. She knows that she is not going to wear it anywhere, but she just wants to possess it. For that she looks at her budget and decides to do away with watching movies for the next two years. Her neighbor Mrs. Butterfield protests, "but it is Marilyn Monroe, my dear," but Mrs. Harris is adamant. This money saved is for her Dior dress.

The story is very heartwarming, but it talks about how many of us are willing to sacrifice on pictures, books, education, travel, etc. in order to indulge in luxuries like gourmet meals, and expensive house, or elaborate clothing.

If you have the willpower to do that, here is my 10% bank account Tip.

The 10% Bank Account

Saving or investment is an item that should appear in every budget. No matter how small the income, etc. when illness or temporary stress on your finances makes saving impossible. Thrift means managing your affairs in such a way that you increase your possessions. Money, land and investment in stocks and shares are just not the only ways in which you can increase your investments. There is a difference between thriftiness and miserly-ness.

Being overly careful about each penny in an unhealthy manner is being miserly. Thriftiness means being careful about money.

This is where the 10% bank account comes in. Now just imagine that you have $500 coming in every month. 10% of this is $50. Shut your eyes, take a deep breath, because hey, you need every cent to pay all your bills and put those $50 in your 10% bank account.

Believe me, this is going to be very painful in the initial stages. That is because we have $500 in hand and we intend to spend all of those dollars. That unfortunately is the innate tendency of mankind, the moment he has some money in hand, unless he is naturally thrifty/miserly.

Now, once that is done – forget about it. Yes, you know that in your subconscious, there is the thought of those $50 lurking and beckoning to you. But you need to be self disciplined. Forget About It.

You are now going to make your whole budget using the remaining $450.

I learned this from one of my uncles who started this 10% business early. As a child, he used to put 10% of his pocket money in an ice cream box in the fridge. That box was, of course, never touched by anybody else, because it was his box. When he wanted something he would take the box out and wait for it to defreeze. By the time the box was defrosted, he would have either changed his mind about buying that item and back would go the box into the freezer again or he would remove just that amount of money necessary to buy that item.

Needless to say, by the time he was a teenager, he had his money working for him and he had taught me his first rule about making money.

When I was around 22, I asked him how to invest money so that it would grow. His advice to me was – make your first million, and after that that million is going to make more millions for you. By the age of 26, I had done that through judicial investment and proper financial planning. By the age of 30, I had spent it all in riotous living, but what a way to go! So I had to go back to work again!

The moral of the story is if you have some money in hand, stick to it. Trips all over the compass and just splashing money around, may be all very fine, and ego boosting, but once the money is gone, it is gone. But if I had invested that money in a good long term deposit it would have multiplied about three times by now.

So, start up your 10% bank account right now. And survive with the rest of the money in your hand. Let your 10% be your passive income and your retirement plan. Do not be silly enough to spend it all in one glorious trip to Paris, because that means that all these years of saving has been for naught. Memories are always fine for the sentimental, but when you are old, you are going to survive on memories, are you?

Making an Household Account

The portion of your annual budget that is spent in any one month is going to depend on the season. You may find costs going up in the winter, because of extra expenditure in fuel costs to heat up the house and clothing for the family.

So, one tip here – once your children have stopped growing, buy all their winter clothing, once and for all.

Make your house account under different headings – on one side you are going to write Source of Income. This is going to include your salary, wages, and allowing, rent, or income from other investments. Make up a total. Take out 10% of this and put it in your 10% account.

Now, with the rest of the money, start buying the necessary items needed for your household. Write down their costs. Also put in the amounts expended for the payments of bills. Make up a sum total at the bottom of the column.

You may also want to make a separate column for charged accounts. This is a danger point for a large number of us, because once we get our credit cards in our hands, we go haywire. If these are kept low, money is going to be saved. I would suggest making sure that your credit card bills should never **exceed more than 10%** of your credit card limit.

What is the fun of having a credit card, if you need to restrict yourself in this manner, you may say. Well, just imagine that you have a $3000 card limit. What would you rather let your bank recover from you, $3000 at the end of the month or $300 [10%?]

Hey, you say, you have been afford it. If you have a $3000 card limit, you are going to go the pace. Well, good for you. But look around you. How many of you are suffering from credit card crunch? How many of you need to talk to your bank manager because you could not pay your credit card bills and then you had to go through a financial meeting with your creditors and a suitable payment system worked out on a given amount of interest every month.

All this hassle could have been avoided if you had just left your credit card at home. But this is one thing we definitely are not going to do, especially when we are in the mood to shop for overpriced things to soothe our own sense of achievement and ego .

To find your financial condition at any time, get the difference between your total expenses and the money received. If there are $60 under charges and $60 under cash expended, you have spent 120 dollars. But if the income coming in is hundred dollars, you are in a debt of $20. Do not get into a debt, as far as possible.

In short, follow the Mr. Micawber principle –*Annual income twenty pounds, annual expenditure nineteen pounds nineteen and six, result happiness. Annual income twenty pounds, annual expenditure twenty pounds nought and six, result misery.*

You mean to tell me you spent this month's budget money on partying with your mates?

Hey, I could not help it. It was Saturday night and all that jazz, you know.

Proper Marketing

It is very sensible to do all your marketing, which not only means the purchase of necessary supplies as meat and vegetables, but also the basic staples of managing a household, by shopping in a store, yourself. That is the only way in which you can know the quality of good articles of the same class, and compare them by weight and price.

Do not do your shopping on your telephone. We have a friendly neighborhood departmental store, just across the road. But it being winter, I decided to ring up the manager so that he would send some household items through his errand boy. While reading out the list, I asked for an item which, according to me, gave good quality for the price. And he said "hmmmmmm." Naturally, I had to ask why he was humming like a bee.

His answer was that the quality of the products of the company to which I was referring had deteriorated so much, even though they had increased their prices, because they were still relying on their brand-name. Instead, he would want to suggest another company, which gave really good quality items at a very reasonable price.

Now, how many store managers are going to give you that sort of advice, especially when I found the other product really excellent? There are so many brand names out there, relying on their name to get through passing off low-quality items or slip-shoddy workmanship. But the consumer is getting to be very aware of such brands.

So the next time you go shopping, make sure that you have time on hand. That is because you are going to do comparative shopping. I remember a friend who really enjoyed shopping, even though most men do not like grocery shopping much. Being an engineer, he took a calculator along with him. He would then go pick up an item, check the weight, check the price, and buy the one which gave him good value for money! That is taking things to an extreme, but there are people who like doing this sort of mental mathematics.[1]

Adulterated foods and pure foods are so much a part of our lives, that we spend more time wondering about adulteration than buying pure unadulterated food in the first place.

A food is going to adulterated if it contains any substitute for the substance which supposedly composes that particular food. Adulterated food is going to be colored or coated. Food is normally adulterated to make it cheaper for the manufacturer, and to give him a greater profit than he could make on pure food.

You can consider preserved foods to be adulterated because they are full of preservatives and fillers. For example, you may find many of the sausage products available in the market today with extra fillers like starch and water. This food is not healthy. Nor is it good value for money. In the same way you think that you have bought hundred grams of pure peppercorn, only

---

[1] I did that, when I was young, and all that comes under the category of blatant showing off. So when the bill was still being made, I had the sum total out, and would say it, before the teller could tell it to me, much to the astonishment of other shoppers. They thought me a mathematical genius! Actually it was just lots of legerdemain – the items always had their totals rounded off to the nearest zero! That made mental calculation very easy. Try it.

to find that it has been adulterated with dry papaya seeds. The manufacturer has cheated you. Also you may be paying a product which supposedly has pure maple syrup, but instead of that, the manufacturer made it up with a mixture of cane syrup and maple syrup.

There are a number of mixtures and compounds which are being used extensively by manufacturers and as long as they are shown in the label, they are accepted as preservatives by the FDA. Believe it or not, we are eating more preservatives than natural products. These preservatives include benzoate of soda, salicylic, boric and benzoic acids. Your food should not have any sort of preservatives.

If you find edible items without coloring items, bleachers and preservatives, by them immediately. At least they are not going to harm your family.

A comparative study of your food can be done by picking up a large number of items manufactured by different companies. You want mixed fruit jam. Which company offers you food, which is not colored or bleached. Does it show that the food is pure? Or is it a compound? Compare the prices. Which chemical colors and preservatives have been put in the jams. Have they been written on the label?

Buying for a Large Family

You may want to purchase cereals, dried fruits, and macaroni in bulk during the winter because they are going to be easily preserved in that weather. In warmer climates or in warmer weather, package goods are usually more satisfactory than bulk goods. Consider the condition of the article as well as the price. Note the directions for the care of food products, given on the packages carefully.

If you have room for storage and your family is large, it is cheapest to buy supplies in bulk quantity. But for a small family, only certain articles can be want to advantage in this way. For example, laundry soap, starch, canned fruit and vegetables can be bought in the autumn when the supply is fresh. Sugar and coffee are articles that can be kept for a long time without loss of flavor, or quality. However, potatoes, roasted coffee, tea, and became bolder, desiccated fruits, dried fruits, beans, cereals and flour begin to deteriorate if they are kept long.

Staple supplies should be purchased for a month. Keep your pantry well-stocked with seasonings, flavorings and even canned goods as are needed for regular use, or for unexpected guests are small emergences .

I remember a 1906 Advertisement for Campbell soups[2] when plutocratic and gourmet uncle George dropped in unexpectedly on his nephew and niece in law and decided to stay for dinner. And it was the cook's day off and the lady told her husband despairingly that he *knew* she could not cook and she was not expected to, being the lady of the house and all. So her enterprising husband just told her to take out some Campbell canned tins, and heat them on the chafing dish and they would do very well. I am sure they did. Today we are going to dine off Campbell beans and chili, while uncle George was fed Pate and pieces of salmon, minced meat and vegetables.

So if you are not doing your own canning and preserving we can always save goodly amounts of money by keeping canned and bottled goods ready at hand.

[2] Saturday evening Post, April, 1906.

Canned and bottled goods are an always welcome mainstay for people on limited budgets.

The Gardeners Pantry

Storing Away Food You Grow for the Winter

COUNTRY LIFE BOOKS

JD-Biz Publishing

Darla Noble

Mendon Cottage Books

Doing the Math

Even for a small family, It is good economy to buy carefully and sometimes in large quantities, because these items are going to be used up sometime or the other.

For example, if a certain package is offered in the market for $.15 per package and you can get the same package into two for $.25, buy the pack of two if you can use them up. Hey, it is just a saving of $.10, you may say, but as they said so often, a Penny saved is a penny earned. Is that not the reason why so many people positively enjoy cutting discount coupons.

Even today, many supermarkets and departmental stores give you a weekly discount, because they are taking out their profits when labeling the goods, which they bought wholesale.[3] at throwaway prices.

The money saved on each package may seem to be a small saving, but in terms of percent, it is going to amount to 16 2/3% or, 4 1/6th of the whole.

Just a little bit of careful buying is going to earn all those easy pennies and cents saved with a little bit here and a little bit there.

In buying canned goods, a reduction is often obtained by taking a dozen cans or a case at a time. Remember to make sure that you read the expiry date of those canned goods. I remember one of my friends going completely haywire, telling us to forget about our lunch hour, because there was a heavy discount on Tropica juices and she was going to buy them.

I definitely do not like concentrated items filled up with preservatives, so I had to rain on her parade. Did you see the expiry date? I asked, and she gave me a look of sheer murder, but she just went to investigate. The expiry date

---

[3] I remember my two-year stint as a sales and purchase Marketing management trainee in a departmental store, more than 30 years ago. I used to get those items wholesale. Then my boss/trainer used to tell me – put the price on it. 75% higher. Now We Are Going to Sell It on the Holiday – 40% discount sales.

All those items sold out within the next three hours.

of those discounted goods were just two months away. So next time you see something which is heavily discounted, you may want to wonder why they are giving away such a free meal? They are definitely not Santa Clauses nor are they altruistic.

You may want to buy things wholesale, especially when you are buying organic fruit from farmers selling their own produce, without benefit of the middleman. A whole basket of fresh fruit and vegetables such as tomatoes and peaches can be purchased for little more than the price of a small quantity of them available in the market. If a whole basket is more than is needed for immediate use, you can preserve the surplus by cooking it and canning it.

Recognizing Your Money Problems

There is nothing more irritating than a know it all who knows everything about how he manages to keep his spending within limits and within the budget, and tells you that at every opportunity.

Many people who have money problems believe that not having enough of monies that primary problem. They are unable to pinpoint their specific difficulties. Other people have a problem with accepting the fact that it is their own bad financial management that has brought about possible financial ruin to the family.

I know of a female who positively revels in the declaration of she really does not have any financial sense and she really could not manage money, because she did not learn how to. Besides, it was the job of the men of the family to keep the females away from financial matters and it was not her job to look after finances.

When she repeated this the third time I lost my cool and told her that she must be really proud of the fact that she is so dumb that she cannot add 2+2. She was really indignant. How could I say that to her? So if not that, she must be proud of the fact that she is not capable of learning how to manage your finances. Even more indignation. What did I mean by that?

When I told her that she was being so proud of the fact that she being a woman meant that she was not needed to bother about finances, she stopped talking to me. Well, ladies, we are definitely not living in Victorian and Edwardian times where we need to ask our menfolk about allowances and leave the financial management to them. That sort of jellyfish behavior has gone out with the crinoline.

So learn how to identify your financial problems. If you cannot add 2+2, get a calculator, but stop being a jellyfish. Here are the difficulties that you do not wish to face.

You cannot balance your checks with the income coming in –

For this you need to keep a tight hold on your spending.

You keep misplacing your bills or lose them –

Just buy a number of sticky tags and stick your bills on the refrigerator. Once they are paid put them away in a file. Your refrigerator's surface should be totally bare by the end of the week.

Many individuals get into financial troubles because they lose money, bills and checkbooks and cannot find the necessary papers at tax time, or just do not know how to plan. This disorganization is no different than the general "disorganization" of the individual's mental state.

To avoid misplacing or losing your financial group is, have a special place in your house where all these papers are stored.

Buy some divider files with the file names written on them. And then remember to file away the required papers in the appropriate file. Your electricity bill is not going to be filed with your insurance papers, because hey, that file was topmost. And you were in a hurry.

Money papers are going to include checkbooks, bills, bank settlements, insurance papers, legal papers, and checks.

You may want to color code the files, so that you can see them at a glance, and file the relevant papers in them when necessary and after they have been dealt with.

Do not put in any bill which has not been paid in a file. Write **paid on** with the date very clearly on each and every bill after the payment has been done. Good managers are able to open up a file even after a period of three years and tell you when they paid for electricity bill for the month of April.

You indulge in impulsive spending or buying things on a whim –

Never go shopping with a friend. She is going to go squealing, how lovely those Donna Karans or Manilo Blahniks are, and you are just going to buy them to prove to her that you can buy them. Even though you never wear them, because they were not in your size.[4]

Being unable to save for long-term projects like a vacation, children's education or retirement –

One does not bother about these things in one's 20s or 30s. However, this should be a top priority when one crosses 30.

Not keeping track of checkbook balances

_____

[4] I have seen that happening. There was this habitual squealer who tagged along with everyone who went shopping and they came back laden with shopping packages and their budget gone out of the window.

Now this was something which even I – who should have known better being an ex-banker – am occasionally guilty. But it is only when my father taught me to write down the balance in my account on top of the checkbook, make out a check and then subtract that amount immediately from the account balance and write it down on the checkbook's front page, that I managed to tackle this particular problem. So do not say that you are going to balance your checkbook on Saturday, when you have the time.

Write out a check. Subtract the balance from your original account amount and write it down in bold letters, right then.

I would suggest recording each monthly expenditure in your checkbook at the beginning of the month, so you will know when they are due. Try eliminating paper arrange for the utilities, mortgage payments and other payments to be automatically withdrawn from your bank account.

Forgetting when your loan payment or mortgage payment is due

Forgetting this important date means that you are subconsciously trying to avoid the responsibility of paying off something which has to be done right away. Procrastination is one of man's biggest failings. If you have this habit, make out a huge chart of **Is Today the 10th? Your mortgage payment is due. Or Is Today the 15th? Did you pay your telephone bill?**

If you think this to be babyish, this is the only way that you can train your mind to accept the fact that you are a responsible person and cannot get away with procrastination. So you have to treat your mind like a baby being disciplined and ordered to do something right now.

Large credit card balances

And then I bought this really beautiful cell phone, and then I decided to go to RITA's to see if there was a discount sale there, and there was there I bought... No, I have not maxed out my credit card yet, but hey, who cares.

The bankers have found another modern way in which they can get hold of your money, by encouraging you to spend, spend, spend. This comes in the form of credit cards. With so many credit cards easily available to you and with you bankers telling you all about payment on attractive terms, is it a surprise that even teenagers has started buying things on credit cards without wondering about how they are going to pay their bills, when they come due?

No wonder so many people are suffering from credit card defaulting problems.

Once, when I was training a banker's workshop on debt consolidation, credit cards and such related items, I lightened the atmosphere by telling all my colleagues and trainees that we bankers were real pirates, weren't we? We just hated the thought of somebody paying his credit card bill in full. That meant that we did not get an opportunity to send him a bill the next month with our percentage stacked on, because he had done the partial payment for the month. With partial payments and interest rates, we could stretch a $200 bill due in January to something like $450 due that October.

When they stopped laughing, they asked me whether I had a credit card and I brought to the house down again by saying, "Perish the thought. My job is getting you to buy a credit card, not buying one for myself!"

So remember that if you have a credit card, either cut it up into small pieces, or keep your credit card expenditure to between 5 – 10% of the credit card limit.

To show you how invidious the lure of the credit card is, that I finally gave in and bought a credit card for myself. And then I just went browsing online. And I fell into temptation, buying things which were going so cheap on eBay UK or eBay USA. Before I knew it, I had passed my self-imposed 10% limit, and gone into the 25% limit in just 20 minutes of crazy buying.

Some items shipped from Hong Kong never arrived, though all the US and UK-based items did in time. So once that happens, one is hooked.

These credit cards are the best promotional source of impulsive spending. They are so convenient to use and that is why so many people are hooked on credit cards. That is why they find it very hard to prioritize their financial commitments.

If you have a large balance on your credit card and do not remember what you purchase your definitely going to be better off without a credit card.

Balances are going to build up rapidly from the interest, late payment fees, and over the limit charges – like I told my trainees! – This accumulation is necessarily going to turn a small purchase into a very large expense.

Paying only the minimum amount due on a large credit card debts means that it is going to take about 30 years to pay off your entire balance. And that is true.

If you are in the habit of not paying off your credit card balances the next time you use your credit card, you would want to ask yourself whether it is really worth paying off the amount on a yellow and black cuddly toy or some branded shoes for the next 30 years?

There are some people with a live in the moment lifestyle which makes them disregard the thought of upcoming and future expenses. These people should never have a credit card in their hand.

So put an interruption between your money and the urge to spend it. Do not look at your ATM machine. Leave your credit card at home. Impulsivity is one of the hallmarks of financial disaster. This is a purchase, you did not plan to make when you left the house that morning. Any purchases that is not part of your budget or any purchases that you did not need is extra impulsive shopping.

Even sensible adults can fall prey to such impulsiveness, occasionally. Do not carry extra cash.

Avoid temptations especially your favorite stores, shopping malls, online websites, home shopping channels and circulars in the newspapers. Throw all the catalogs out as soon as they arrive. Use discount sale pamphlets for making shopping lists instead of buying the items on them. This is good use of extra paper!

Bring this list when you are shopping and stick to it.

Making Good Budget Menus
HEALTHY EATING THROUGH
GOOD PLANNING

MENU

HEALTH LEARNING SERIES

JD-Biz Publishing   Dueep J. Singh

Mendon Cottage Books

Bring a calculator to the store to add up your purchases as they accumulate. You know what your budget is. The moment you find yourself extending your budget, you may want to exchange some of the items in your shopping cart, for less-expensive items.

Do like my uncle did. He waited a certain amount of time before making a purchase. If that time elapsed and he still decided that he wanted to purchase the item, and he had the money to buy it, then he went ahead and bought it. Otherwise, he put the money back into the freezer!

Find things to do which are free and inexpensive. Shopping is now being used as a substitute for entertainment by a number of people all over the world. This is not a healthy trend. These people are now shopaholics. They have no social life because they are always spending money like there is no tomorrow.

There are number of stimulating activities which you can do like visiting parks, joining the nature group, participating in sports, or just walking around the city. As long as you keep away from the market. The moment you decide that you need to shop, and you cannot do without shopping, that means that there is something wrong. This compulsiveness is not healthy and make sure that you do not fall a prey to it.

Conclusion

This book has given you a number of useful tips and suggestions on how you can manage your money successfully. This demands that you be able to account for your money and for your purchases.

Keeping a record of purchases helps curb impulsivity and serves as an indicator of whether you are earning your money where you want to be spending it or towards something which you bought impulsively or just because.

As you track your spending, certain categories will naturally emerge. The categories here are different for each person, but the main categories for cash include groceries, parking, restaurants, coffee shops, snacks, vending machines, cosmetics, newspapers, clothing, household items, books, gasoline and other day-to-day items.

As you continue to record your spending you are not going to wonder where all the money goes.

It may be difficult for adults to write down all of their expenses, but do the best you can try keeping a track of expenses for one week or several weeks. At first this is going to be difficult, and you may need the help of someone in writing down all the expenses. Try dictating them into a small handheld recorder/cell phone to record expenses as messages on your answering machine. Even if you cannot keep a perfect record of every expense, the ones that you do collect are going to help you move forward in changing your money management habits.

So how much did that hamburger and coffee cost?

Here is one last tip for managing your money. Buy a number of different colored envelopes. Write down the necessary budget item labels on every envelope and fill them up with the required amount of money.

Whenever you need to pay the money for one particular item, withdraw the money from the appropriate envelope. When there is no money left in a given envelope of that you have spend the allocated amount for that particular category. That means you are not going to be making any more purchases in that particular category until next month or until you receive your next paycheck.

Using an envelope system means that you are going to be spending the exact amount of money for that particular utility when required.

If you are suffering from a debt problem, you may want to talk to your creditors. Ask them for a lower percentage rate or a reduced late fees. Arrange regular payments with creditors and stick to the plan. Do not promise more than you can pay reasonably and realistically. Your creditors are less likely to cooperate, if you do not keep promises, or you do not stick to what you have agreed to pay monthly.

This book is for all those people who want to know how to keep within the budget and realistically. So try implementing these tips right now, live long and prosper!

Author Bio

Dueep Jyot Singh is a Management and IT Professional who managed to gather Postgraduate qualifications in Management and English and Degrees in Science, French and Education while pursuing different enjoyable career options like being an hospital administrator, IT,SEO and HRD Database Manager/ trainer, movie , radio and TV scriptwriter, theatre artiste and public speaker, lecturer in French, Marketing and Advertising, ex-Editor of Hearts On Fire (now known as Solstice) Books Missouri USA, advice columnist and cartoonist, publisher and Aviation School trainer, ex-moderator on Medico.in, banker, student councilor ,travelogue writer … among other things!

One fine morning, she decided that she had enough of killing herself by Degrees and went back to her first love—writing. It's more enjoyable! She already has 48 published academic and 14 fiction- in- different- genre books under her belt.

When she is not designing websites or making Graphic design illustrations for clients , she is browsing through old bookshops hunting for treasures, of which she has an enviable collection – including R.L. Stevenson, O.Henry, Dornford Yates, Maurice Walsh, De Maupassant, Victor Hugo, Sapper, C.N. Williamson, "Bartimeus" and the crown of her collection- Dickens "The Old Curiosity Shop," and so on… Just call her "Renaissance Woman") - collecting herbal remedies, acting like Universal Helping Hand/Agony Aunt, or escaping to her dear mountains for a bit of exploring, collecting herbs and plants and trekking.

Check out some of the other JD-Biz Publishing books

Gardening Series on Amazon

Country Life Books

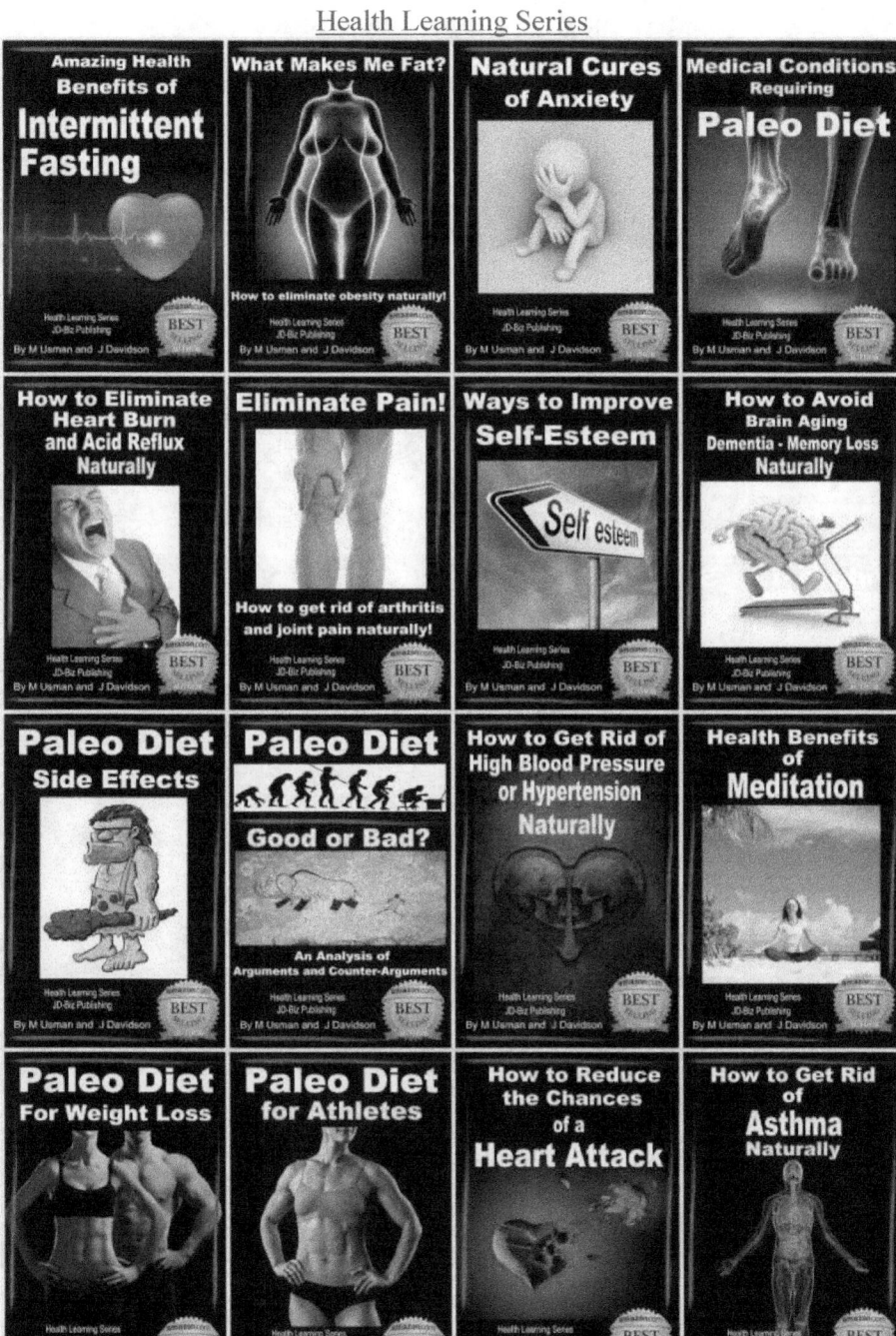

Amazing Animal Book Series

How to Build and Plan Books

Entrepreneur Book Series

Our books are available at

1. Amazon.com

2. Barnes and Noble

3. Itunes

4. Kobo

5. Smashwords

6. Google Play Books

Publisher

JD-Biz Corp

P O Box 374

Mendon, Utah 84325

http://www.jd-biz.com/

Mendon Cottage Books

P O Box 374, Mendon Utah 84325

Mendon Cottage Books